Trivia and Fun Facts
for
Smart and Curious Kids

Regina Mathis

'Dinosaur' means 'terrible lizard' in Greek.

'Dreamt' is the only English word that ends in the letters 'mt'.

'Stewardesses' is the longest word that is typed with only the left hand.

'Typewriter' is the longest word that can be made using only the top row of a keyboard.

20 percent of the food we eat is used to fuel our brain.

A beefalo is a part cow, part bison!

A blue whale's tongue is heavier than an elephant's.

A blue whale's heart can weigh up to 400 pounds-- about 640 times more than a human heart.

A bolt of lightning is five times hotter than the sun!!

A camel's hump stores fat, not water.

A cat has 32 muscles in each ear.

A chameleon can change its color in just 20 seconds.

A chameleon's tongue is at least as long as its body.

A cloud can weigh over one million pounds.

A common garden snail has nearly 14000 teeth!! Astounding, right?

A coyote can hear a mouse moving almost a foot under the snow!!

A crab's taste buds are on their feet.

A crocodile cannot stick its tongue out.

A day on Venus is longer than a year on Venus.

A dime has 118 ridges around the edge.

A flamingo can only eat when its head is upside down.

A fox uses its tail to communicate with other foxes.

A giraffe's heart is two feet long and weighs about 25 pounds.

A giraffe's tongue is so long that it can clean its own ears.

A group of flamingos is called a "flamboyance."

A hippo's lips are nearly two feet wide.

A human body contains almost 100 trillion cells.

A hurricane releases enough energy in one second to equal that of 10 atomic bombs.

A koala's fingerprints are so like human fingerprints that they could taint a crime scene.

A lipogram is a kind of written work where a particular letter is avoided.

A male Ostrich can roar like a Lion! Weird but true...

A neutron star can spin 600 times in one second.

A Nigersaurus has an unusual skull containing as many as 500 slender teeth.

A palindrome is a word that reads the same backward as forward, like 'racecar.'

A pet hamster can run up to 6 miles a night on a wheel.

A prawn's heart is located at the bottom of its head!

A sentence that uses every letter of the alphabet at least once is called a pangram.

A shark is the only known fish that can blink with both eyes.

A shrimp's heart is in its head.

A single human hair can hold the weight of an apple.

A single wind turbine can generate enough electricity to power 1,400 homes.

A snail can sleep for three years.

A Snail's Pace: The average snail moves at a speed of about 0.03 miles per hour.

A sneeze can travel out of your nose at over 100 mph.

AB negative is the rarest blood type.

Abe Lincoln was a professional wrestler long before he became the 16th President of the United States.

About 1,000 new words are added to the English language every year.

About 70% of an adult human body is water.

About 71% of the Earth's surface is covered in water, but only 2.5% of it is fresh water.

About half of your body is bacteria.

Abraham Lincoln – the 16th American President was a licensed bartender.

Abraham Lincoln lost five separate elections before he became president of the U.S. (Never, ever, ever give up!)

Abraham Lincoln stood at 6 feet 4 inches making him one of the tallest U.S. presidents.

According to Google data, there are 129,864,880 unique books in the world!

According to Tori Avey, coffee became a popular drink in America after the Boston Tea Party of 1773.

Africa is the only continent that covers all four hemispheres.

Alaska is both the most western and the most eastern state in the United States.

Alaska is the largest state in the U.S. by area.

Alaska is the state with the longest coastline.

All cheese is naturally white, off-white, or golden yellow.

All clownfish are born male. They are able change their sex later on and that change is irreversible!!

Alpha Centauri isn't a star, but a star system. It is 4.22 lightyears away.

Amazon is the biggest river in the world and carries one-fifth of all the river water on Earth.

Amelia Earhart first saw a plane at the age of 10 but didn't take an airplane ride until 1920 when she was 23 years old.

Americans eat about 20 billion hot dogs a year, often at baseball games.

An anagram is a word or phrase formed by rearranging the letters of another, like 'listen' and 'silent.'

An avalanche can travel up to the speed of 80 mph!

An average yawn is nearly six seconds long.

An elephant is the largest land mammal.

An elephant's foot is so designed that when they walk, they are technically always on tiptoe.

An elephant's trunk has over 40,000 muscles.

An ostrich's eye is bigger than its brain.

Ancient Egyptians had more than 2,000 deities whom they worshipped!

Ancient Greeks believed redheads become vampires after death!

Ancient Romans watched gladiator fights and other events at the Colosseum in Rome.

Ancient Rome not only had male gladiators but also female gladiators?! A female gladiator was called a Gladiatrix, or Gladiatrices.

Antarctic desert is the largest desert in the world and is referred to as the Polar desert.

Antarctica is the only continent with no permanent human residents.

Anteaters have no teeth! Weird but true!

Ants can carry objects 50 times their own body weight.

Apples are in the rose family.

Apples float because they are one-quarter air!

Applesauce was the first food eaten in space by astronauts.

Armored Dinosaur: The Ankylosaurus had bony plates all over its body for protection.

Astronaut Alan Shepard hit a golf ball on the Moon in 1971.

Astronauts say the moon smells like spent gunpowder.

At least 12 rocks from planet Mars have landed on Earth.

Atacama Desert, Chile is the world's driest place with less than 1mm of annual average precipitation.

Australia is home to 11 per cent of the world's 6,300 reptile species making it the continent with the greatest number of reptiles!

Avocados, tomatoes, and cucumbers are fruits.

Babe Ruth began his career as a pitcher: Ruth was both a left-handed pitcher and a left-handed batter.

Babe Ruth was the first baseball player to hit a home run in the All-Star game, at Chicago's Comiskey Park in 1933.

Babies are born with about 300 bones, but adults have only 206 as some fuse.

Baby elephants suck their trunks like human babies suck their thumbs for comfort.

Bananas are curved because they grow towards the sun.

Bananas are naturally radioactive due to potassium.

Bananas are technically berries, while strawberries are not.

Bananas contain a chemical (tryptophan) that can make you feel happy and relaxed.

Baseball is known as America's pastime.

Baseballs last an average of seven pitches.

Basketball was invented in 1891 by James Naismith using peach baskets as hoops.

Bats are the only mammals that can fly.

Bats use echolocation to navigate and find food in the dark.

Bees are found everywhere in the world apart from Antarctica.

Bees can make blue honey if they eat certain types of fruit.

Bees can see the color ultraviolet, which is invisible to humans.

Bees communicate by dancing and using different sounds.

Before 1913, parents could mail their kids to their grandparents through postal services. Mailed to your grandparents' house?

Before becoming the 40th American President, Ronald Wilson Reagan served as a lifeguard and saved around 77 people from drowning!

Before European contact (caused populations to diminish rapidly) California indigenous tribal groups spoke more than 200 unique dialects.

Before modern goggles, swimmers used to put jelly on their eyes to see underwater.

Believe it or not – In Wales, United Kingdom, it is possible to compete in an underwater mountain bike race!!

Believe it or not but some cars can run on used French fries oil!

Believe it or not but the Dead Sea is actually a saltwater lake!

Believe it or not, Caterpillars have 12 eyes!!

Biggest Carnivore: The Spinosaurus is considered the largest carnivorous dinosaur.

Bill Clinton has two Grammy Awards.

Black Death wiped out nearly 75 million Europeans, that's more than one-third of Europe's population, in the Middle Ages!

Black holes have such strong gravity that not even light can escape from them.

Blackbird's Rainbow: A raven's feathers can sometimes show a rainbow of colors in sunlight.

Blue, red, and yellow are primary colors — these colors plus white and black blend to make all other colors.

Both the width and the height of the Gateway Arch in St. Louis are 630 feet.

Brown eyes are the most prevalent in the human population.

Butterflies taste with their feet and their wings are made of tiny scales.

Can you believe pork rinds were a favorite renaissance snack!

Canada and the United States of America share the longest international border, which spans about 8,890 km.

Carbon dioxide is a gas we can't see or smell, but it's important for plants to make food.

Carrots weren't always orange: they were once exclusively purple.

Cat urine glows under a black-light.

Caterpillars have 12 eyes!

Caterpillars turn into a liquid inside the cocoon before becoming a butterfly.

Cats are often scared of cucumbers because they mistake them for snakes.

Cats can't taste anything that is sweet.

Ceres is the only dwarf planet that sits in the asteroid belt, which stretches between Mars and Jupiter!

Certain types of spiders can fly or 'parachute' using their webs, traveling long distances through the air.

Chameleons change their color based on their mood, temperature, and light.

Cheese is a dairy! It is the resulting product of curdling milk

Cheese was accidentally discovered by carrying milk in the stomach linings of animals. The bacteria rennet contained there curdles milk.

Cherries are a member of the rose family (Rosaceae) as are quince, pears, plums, apples, peaches, and raspberries!

Chickens can be hypnotized by drawing a line in front of their beaks.

Ching Shih is believed to be the world's most successful pirate in history and was a woman!

Cilantro and coriander are considered to be the same.

Cleopatra wasn't Egyptian—she
was Greek.

Cleopatra, the last pharaoh of
Egypt, could speak at least seven
languages.

Clever Girl: Velociraptors were very
smart and could hunt in packs.

Clouds aren't weightless, they can
weigh over a million pounds.

Clouds look white because they are reflecting sunlight from above them.

Cockroaches can live for a week without their heads!

Congo River, Zaire is the deepest river of the world with a depth of 219.5m!

Continent of Antarctica has no countries! Weird but true!

Coral reefs can be heard 'singing' as the fish and other creatures create noises.

Cows can sense Earth's magnetic field and usually graze facing north or south.

Cows can walk up the stairs by themselves but can't get down without help!

Cows have four stomachs to digest food!

Crocodiles really do cry, but not from emotions; it's to clean their eyes.

Crows can recognize human faces.

Cuba and North Korea are the only countries in the world where you cannot buy or sell Coca-Cola.

Curling stones are made from rare granite found only in Scotland and Wales.

D River in Oregon, USA is the shortest river in the world. It is only 37 m long.

Did you know a grizzly bear can run as fast as a horse?

Did you know a hippopotamus can run faster than a man?

Did you know an ostrich's brain is smaller than it's eye!!

Did you know Easter always falls between March 22 and April 25?!

Did you know Easter Island houses 887 giant head statues that were carved nearly 2000 years ago?!

Did you know Elephants are the only animals that can't jump!

Did you know If you could travel at the speed of light, you would never get any older?!

Did you know it was popular for Viking men to dye their hair blonde?! Some went further and even dyed their beards!

Did you know Monkeys can go bald in old age, just like humans?!

Did you know Neptune has the fastest winds in the solar system? Its winds reach an astonishing speed of 1600 mph!

Did you know one day on Venus is almost as long as 8 months on Earth?

Did you know Panda droppings could be recycled into paper!

Did you know people made clothes out of food sacks during the Great Depression?

Did you know Pluto got its name from an 11-year-old girl, Venetia Burney of Oxford?

Did you know rubber bands last longer when refrigerated?!

Did you know Shark does not have bones? Instead, its skeleton is made of cartilage.

Did you know slugs have four noses?!

Did you know some perfumes actually have whale poop in them? Weird but true!

Did you know some salamanders can regrow their tails, legs, even parts of their eyes?

Did you know that you can estimate the temperature of a place by the number of times some crickets chirp in a second? Weird but true!!

Did you know the Eiffel Tower grows taller every summer and shrinks back in winter?!

Did you know theatre was invented by ancient Greeks?!

Did you know there are nearly 2,000 thunderstorms on Earth every minute?

Did you know you are as tall as the length of your arms stretched out?

Did you know you use 200 different muscles in the body to walk?!

Dino Colors: Scientists believe some dinosaurs were brightly colored, not just gray and green.

Dino Footprints: Paleontologists find dinosaur footprints as well as bones, which tell us how they moved.

Dino Relatives: Birds are the closest living relatives to dinosaurs.

Dino Teeth: Some dinosaurs, like the Hadrosaurus, had over 1,000 teeth!

Dinosaur eggs weren't all huge; some were as small as a chicken's egg.

Dinosaur fossils have been found on all seven continents.

Disney World in Florida is the most visited vacation resort in the world.

Dogs can hear 10 times better than humans!

Dogs can smell nearly 100,000 times better than humans!!

Dogs have two different air passages, one for breathing and one for smelling.

Dolphins have been seen wrapping sea sponges around their long snouts to protect them.

Dolphins have names for each other and call out for each other specifically.

Dolphins have their own language and can talk to each other.

During the Victorian era, it was popular for people to take photographs of their loved ones after they had died.

During volcanic eruptions, lightning can strike in the ash cloud, a phenomenon known as 'dirty thunderstorms.'

Early high jumpers used to land on their feet instead of their backs.

Earth is not shaped like a perfect sphere as some believe. It bulges out at the equator looking more like a "squished ball".

Earth is the fifth largest planet in our solar system.

Earth is the third planet from the sun.

Elephants are one of the few animals that can recognize themselves in a mirror.

Elvis Presley was one of the largest private donors to the Pearl Harbor memorial.

Europa, one of Jupiter's moons, has saltwater geysers that are 20x taller than Mt. Everest.

Even in an airplane, a trip to Pluto would take about 800 years.

Every dog's nose and paw print is unique – much like a human fingerprint!

Every minute, your entire blood passes through your heart!

Extinction Mystery: It's believed a giant asteroid impact caused the dinosaurs to become extinct.

Eyelashes live for about 150 days before falling out.

Fast Runners: The Compsognathus could run up to 40 mph.

Female hummingbirds build the world's smallest bird's nest, about the size of a walnut!

Female lions do about 90% of the hunting.

Fingernails can grow 4x faster than toenails.

Fireflies glow to attract a mate and to scare away predators.

Flamingos are pink because they eat pink shrimp!

Footprints on the Moon can last for 100 million years! Weird but true...

Formula 1 cars can go from 0 to 60 mph in just 2.6 seconds.

Franklin D. Roosevelt is the only American president to have served more than two terms.

Frederick Douglass taught himself to read and write.

French fries are Belgian, not French.

Frida Kahlo created 143 paintings. Of these, 55 were self-portraits.

Frogs can be made to float in mid-air using magnets.

Garlic bulbs are full of Vitamin C, iron, potassium, magnesium, zinc, and more. It also has 17 amino acids.

Geckos can stick to surfaces because their feet have tiny hairs that create a strong adhesive force.

George Washington didn't chop down a cherry tree.

George Washington opened a whiskey distillery after his presidential term.

George Washington was the first President of the United States.

George Washington, Thomas Jefferson, Theodore Roosevelt and Abraham Lincoln are the four presidents on Mount Rushmore.

German chocolate cake is not from Germany. German is actually the last name of the man who invented a kind of baking chocolate.

Ginko Biloba is the oldest living tree species, at around 250 million years old.

Glass is made from sand and can be transparent or colored.

Goats have rectangular pupils to give them a wide field of vision.

Golden Sunsets: The sun can appear red, orange, or golden during sunsets due to the scattering of light.

Golf is one of only two sports ever played on the moon. The other sport was javelin toss.

Gorilla's burp when they are happy! Gouda cheese accounts for 50-60% of the world's consumption of cheese.

Grasshoppers have been known to turn pink in certain environmental conditions.

Gravity on the Moon is only 1/6th of Earth's, so you can jump higher there.

Gray Matters: Koalas have fingerprints similar to humans, and they're a gray color.

Great white sharks are the largest predatory fish and can grow up to 19 feet long.

Green Eggs, Anyone? Emu eggs are naturally green.

Greenland is the largest island in the world.

Ham the Astrochimp was the first hominid in space!

Hawaii is home to some of the world's most active volcanoes.

Hawaii is the only U.S. state made entirely of islands.

Hedy Lamar was a famous Hollywood film actress who also invented what became modern-day Wi-Fi.

Herbivore Defense: Some herbivorous dinosaurs had sharp spikes or horns to protect themselves from predators.

Herbivore Giants: The Apatosaurus, a plant-eater, was as long as two school buses.

Hippo sweat is pink and works as an effective sunscreen.

Historic Route 66 was one of the original U.S. highways, famous for road trips.

Hollywood in California is considered the movie capital of the world.

Honey is the only food that doesn't go bad.

Honeybees can fly at speeds of up to 15 miles per hour.

Honeybees flap their wings 230 times every second.

Honeybees perform a 'waggle dance' to tell other bees the direction and distance to flowers with nectar.

Hot water freezes faster than cold water.

Human bodies give off a tiny amount of light that is too weak for our eyes to see.

Human eyes are made of nearly 2 million working parts.

Human Eyes can detect about 10 million different colors!

Human teeth are as strong as shark teeth!

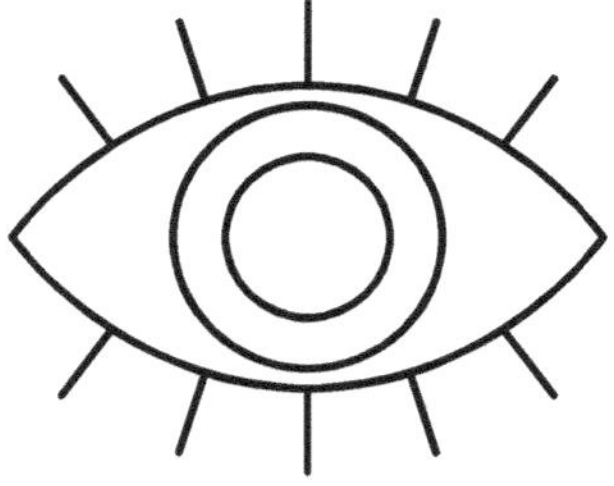

Humans are the only animals with chins.

Humans have around 10,000 taste buds, and they're replaced every 2 weeks.

Hummingbirds are the only birds that can fly literally every direction and hover in mid-air.

Ice cream was once called "cream ice."

Ice hockey started as an indoor sport in Montreal in 1875.

Ice is less dense than water, which is why ice cubes float in your drink.

Iceland is the biggest volcanic island in the world.

If all of the ice in Antarctica melted, the world's oceans would rise by about 200 feet.

If you sneeze too hard, you could fracture a rib.

If you soak an egg in vinegar, the shell becomes rubbery and bouncy.

If you would unwrap an Egyptian Mummy, it's bandages can stretch up to 1.6km! Weird but true...

Iguazu Falls, in Argentina and Brazil, is the largest waterfall system in the world. It spans nearly 3 km and has 275 vertical drops!

In 1588, the Spanish Armada was defeated by the English, changing the balance of power in Europe.

In 1919, Cleveland Indians pitcher Ray Caldwell was struck by lightning in the middle of the 9th inning. He kept playing!

In 1920, American women won the right to vote with the 19th Amendment.

In 1961, Yuri Gagarin of Soviet Union became the first man in outer space.

In 1962, Wilt Chamberlain scored 100 points in a single NBA basketball game. No one has broken this record (not even Steph Curry!).

In 1969, Neil Armstrong was the first human to walk on the moon.

In 1971, a tennis match was played on the wings of two flying airplanes.

In 1998, a baseball was flown aboard the Space Shuttle Discovery.

In 2011, 10-year-old Kathryn Aurora Gray discovered a supernova (a star out of energy, explodes, and then collapses before it dies).

In a lifetime, the average person produces enough saliva to fill two swimming pools.

In Antarctica, there's a waterfall called Blood Falls, where red water flows.

In Barrow, Alaska, the sun doesn't set for around 82 days in summer.

In Brazil, there's a river wave called Pororoca that can last for up to half an hour.

In certain parts of the world, fireflies synchronize their flashing.

In Death Valley, rocks move across the desert floor leaving trails, but nobody has seen them move.

In English, the letter 'Q' is almost always followed by the letter 'U.'

In Honduras, there's a phenomenon where fish rain from the sky, known as 'Lluvia de Peces.'

In India, people have been guiding tree roots to grow into natural bridges for centuries.

In many advertisements, the time displayed on a watch is 10:10.

In Panama, there's a forest with trees that have square trunks.

In space, astronauts experience zero gravity and float inside their spacecraft.

In the 14th century, the Black Death killed approximately one-third of Europe's population.

In the Canary Islands, there's a whistling language used to communicate across vast valleys.

In the desert, rocks can be naturally sculpted into bizarre shapes by the wind.

In the wild, some reindeer travel more than 3000 miles in a single year.

In the wintertime reindeer grow their facial hair long enough to cover their mouths, which protects their muzzles when grazing in the snow. Beard-os!

In Venezuela, there's a place where lightning strikes almost 300 nights a year.

In winter, methane gas freezes in lakes, creating beautiful patterns of bubbles under the ice.

In your lifetime, at sleep, you might eat 70 assorted insects and 10 spiders, or more!

India was the only source of diamonds till 1896!

It can be too warm to snow, but never too cold.

It has snowed in the Sahara Desert, one of the hottest places on Earth.

It is illegal to stand within 90 metres of distance from the Queen without socks on.

It is impossible for most people to lick their own elbow. (try it!)

It takes about 10 pounds of milk to make 1 pound of cheese.

It takes eight minutes and 19 seconds for light to travel from the Sun to Earth.

It takes Jupiter only 10 hours to complete a rotation around its axis, making it the fastest spinning planet in the solar system.

It takes the Earth about 24 hours to rotate once on its axis.

It takes the human body about 12 hours to digest food after it's been eaten.

It would take 70,000 years in the fastest spaceship to reach the Alpha Centauri! That's how far it is!

It's impossible to sneeze with your eyes open.

It's physically impossible for pigs to look up into the sky... weird but true!

James Webb Telescope is the largest space telescope in the world with a primary mirror diameter of 6.5 meters!

Jazz music originated in the United States in the early 20th century.

Joan of Arc, a teenage girl, led the French army to victory over the English in 1429.

Johannes Gutenberg invented the printing press in the 15th century, revolutionizing the way books were made.

Judo was first included in the Olympics in 1964 in Tokyo.

Jupiter's Great Red Spot is a storm that has been raging for over 200 years.

Jurassic Period: There are three major periods when dinosaurs lived. The famous Jurassic period, the Triassic and Cretaceous periods.

Just like human fingerprints, every cat's nose print is unique.

Just like humans, bats have belly buttons.

Kangaroos can't walk backwards and use their tails for balance when hopping.

Kansas City, Missouri, has more fountains than any other city in the world besides Rome.

Kelp forests underwater can grow up to 18 inches in a single day.

Lake Baikal of Russia is the biggest freshwater lake by volume.

Lake Hillier in Australia is naturally pink due to algae.

Largest Desert: The Sahara Desert is the largest hot desert in the world, covering a land area as large as the USA.

Leonardo da Vinci, a famous artist, could write with one hand and draw with the other at the same time.

Light travels at about 186,282 miles per second.

Lightning can be five times hotter than the surface of the sun.

Lightning can, in fact, strike twice.

Lobsters can be blue, yellow, or even two different colors, but they all turn red when cooked.

Los Angeles' full name is 'El Pueblo de Nuestra Senora la Reina de los Angeles de Porciuncula'

Maine is the only state that has a one-syllable name.

Male Gentoo penguins offer the smoothest pebble they can find to their mate.

Manon Rheaume is the only woman to have played in an NHL game.

Many dinosaur fossils have been found in the U.S., including the famous T-Rex.

Many English words have silent letters, like the 'k' in 'knight.'

Many English words originated from Greek and Latin.

Many people think early mermaid sightings can be attributed to dehydration + manatees.

Mardi Gras in New Orleans, Louisiana, is famous for its colorful parades and celebrations.

Martin Luther King Jr. Day is an American federal holiday marking the birthday of Martin Luther King Jr.

Mauna Kea is the highest mountain on the ocean bed at a staggering 10,000m high with nearly 6000m submerged in the Pacific Ocean.

Mauna Loa is the biggest active volcano on Earth.

Mawsynram in Meghalaya, India is the world's rainiest place with an average annual rainfall of 11,871 mm.

Mayan people worshipped turkeys as Gods!! Weird but true...

Men are more likely to be colorblind than women.

Modern Olympic gold medals are mostly made of silver with a gold coating.

Monarch butterflies migrate 3,000 miles from Canada to Mexico every year.

Moonbows or lunar rainbows appear at night and are much rarer than rainbows.

More than 480 million people have played Monopoly.

More than 80% of the world's ocean is unmapped and unexplored.

Most people fall asleep in seven minutes.

Mount Rushmore features the faces of four presidents: Washington, Jefferson, Roosevelt, and Lincoln.

Mount Thor on Baffin Island, Canada, has Earth's greatest vertical drop of 1250 m!

Mystery snails can regenerate their eyes completely after amputation through the mid-eyestalk!

Nearly 10 percent of all of a cat's bones are in its tail.

Nearly 85 percent of all plant life on Earth is found in the ocean.

Neptune's days are 16 hours long.

New Zealand has more sheep than people.

Newborn babies are partially colorblind.

NFL Super Bowl referees also get Super Bowl rings.

Niagara Falls is one of the most famous waterfalls in the world, located between the U.S. and Canada.

No country can own the Moon, according to an international treaty.

No two spots on a whale shark are the same. They are as unique as fingerprints.

Not all pumpkins are orange; some can be white, green, or even blue.

Not only does everyone have unique fingerprints, but humans also have unique tongue prints!

Number four is the only one with the same number of letters!

Octopi have three hearts.

Octopuses can squeeze through tiny openings because they have no bones.

Octopuses have blue blood and nine brains!

Octopuses have blue blood because their blood uses copper for oxygen transport instead of iron.

Olympus Mons is the tallest planetary mountain in the Solar system. It is nearly 2.5 times the Mount Everest's height above sea level.

On average, the human heart beats 100,000 times a day.

On Neptune, the wind blows over 1,000 miles per hour.

On the planet Mercury, days are longer than years on Earth.

On the South Atlantic island of Tristan da Cunha, potatoes were once used as currency.

One day on Venus is almost 8 months on Earth.

One large tree can supply a day's oxygen for up to four people.

One million Earths could fit inside the sun!

One teaspoon of a neutron star would weigh six billion tons.

One-quarter of your bones are in your feet.

Only half of the dolphin's brain goes to sleep when asleep and the other half stays awake.

Orange Oranges? Not all oranges are orange; some are green even when ripe.

Originally, frozen cow dung was used as hockey pucks in the early days of ice hockey.

Oscar Swahn, 72, is the oldest person to win an Olympic medal.

Ostriches can run faster than horses.

Other than humans, emperor penguins are the only warm-blooded animal to stay in Antarctica for the winter.

Our nose is a natural lie detector... it gets warmer as we lie! Weird but true!

Over 1 billion hours of YouTube videos are watched every day! That's more than the amount of Netflix and Facebook videos combined!

Owls can't move their eyeballs!

Pablo Picasso entered art school around age 10. The Picasso Museum in Barcelona, Spain includes many "early works" from his childhood.

Paper was first invented in ancient China.

Peanuts aren't nuts! (They're legumes.)

Penguins are considered marine animals.

Penguins can jump up to 6 feet in the air when they waddle.

Penguins have a special bone in their wrist to help them 'fly' underwater.

Penguins huddle together to stay warm in extreme cold.

Pineapples take two years to grow.

Pineapples were a status symbol in 18th century England! Weird but true...

Pink Dolphins: There are pink dolphins called Amazon River Dolphins.

Plants can send distress signals to other plants when they're under attack.

Plants use sunlight to make their own food in a process called photosynthesis.

Plastic Pollution: Every year, about 8 million tons of plastic waste is dumped into the world's oceans.

Point Nemo in the South Pacific Ocean is the farthest point from land on Earth. It is 2688 km away from the nearest landmass.

Porcupines can float.

Potatoes were the first vegetable to be grown in space.

Pound cake is so-called because the recipes once called for a pound of butter, a pound of sugar, a pound of eggs, and a pound of flour.

Presently, over 700 dinosaurs have been identified and named.

President Theodore Roosevelt is responsible for giving The White House its name.

Proxima Centauri is the nearest
star to the Earth.

Pterosaurs were flying reptiles that
lived during the time of dinosaurs.

Pumice stone, a type of igneous
rock, is so light that it floats in
water.

Purple was once a royal color, so
expensive only kings and queens
could afford it.

Pyura chilensis is a sea creature that looks like a rock but has blood and a heart.

Rain contains vitamin B12.

Rainbows are made when light is bent and reflected in raindrops.

Rats laugh when being tickled.

Recycling one ton of paper can save 17 trees and 7,000 gallons of water.

Red Alert! The first color babies can see is red.

Regardless of their size, naval tradition declares submarines to be called "boats" rather than "ships."

Rhode Island is the smallest state in the U.S.

Ripe cranberries will bounce like a ball. (Go on, try it!). They also float.

Robots on Mars send back pictures and data to Earth.

Roses can be dyed to create a rainbow effect on their petals.

Russia is just around 2.5 miles away from Alaska! The distance between Big Diomede (owned by Russia) and Little Diomede (owned by the US)!

Russia ran out of vodka while celebrating the end of World War II! The party lasted for nearly 22 hours.

Sally Ride was the first American woman to fly in space, on June 18, 1983.

Saturn's rings are made from trillions of chunks of orbiting ice.

Scientists aren't sure what sounds dinosaurs made, but they might have roared.

Scientists estimate the Earth is around 4.5 billion years old.

Sea Lions are the only animals that can clap to a beat.

Sea otters hold hands as they sleep. It keeps them from floating away in the sea while they sleep.

Shakespeare invented many words, like 'assassination' and 'bump.'

Sharks can have up to 50,000 teeth in their lifetime.

Sharks do not hunt humans or consider humans food. They hunt for seals, dolphins, etc., and accidentally get humans.

Ships can float on water because they displace enough water to hold their weight.

Silicon Valley in California is the global center for high technology and innovation.

Sir Edmund Hillary and Tenzing Norgay were the first to reach the summit of Mount Everest in 1953.

Skateboarding originated in the 1940s when surfers wanted something to do when the waves were flat.

Sloths are excellent swimmers and can hold their breath for up to forty minutes underwater!

Sloths are strong swimmers, especially good at the backstroke.

Sloths cannot shiver to stay warm, and so have difficulty maintaining their body temperature on rainy days.

Snails take the longest naps with some lasting as long as three years.

Snakes, crocodiles and bees were just a few of the animals who lived alongside dinosaurs.

Soccer is the most popular sport in the world, played by over 250 million people.

Solar Power: Just one hour of sunlight, if harnessed properly, could power the world for a year.

Some beaches glow in the dark due to bioluminescent plankton in the water.

Some desert sands can 'sing' or make noise when the wind blows.

Some dinosaurs laid eggs bigger than a basketball.

Some dinosaurs, like the Velociraptor, had feathers.

Some fish can cough! Weird but true!

Some hummingbirds can weigh less than a penny!

Some lipsticks contain fish scales.

Some mushrooms, like the Mycena chlorophos, glow in the dark.

Some plants in the Arctic circle grow in a spiral shape to absorb more sunlight.

Some plants, like the Venus Flytrap, are carnivores—they eat tiny insects for nutrients.

Some species of ants can glide back to their tree if they fall off a branch.

Some tornadoes can be faster than Formula One race cars!

Some turtles can breathe through their rear ends.

Some turtles can glow in the dark. This bioluminescence is used to ward off predators or attract mates.

Some types of jellyfish are immortal and can revert back to their juvenile form.

Some types of slime mold can find the shortest path through a maze using magnetism.

Sometimes, fish or frogs rain from the sky due to strong winds like tornadoes picking them up.

Spain, Sweden, and Switzerland remained neutral in World War II and did not join any side.

SPAM is a mash-up of the words 'spice' and 'ham'

Spider silk is stronger than steel of the same thickness.

Squid, Octopus, Horseshoe crabs have blue blood!!

Starfish have no brains.

Stonehenge in England is over 5,000 years old, and its purpose is still a mystery.

Strawberries and raspberries wear their seeds on the outside.

Sunset on Mars appears blue!! That's another random fact for kids that is sure to baffle them.

Table tennis helped improve China and America's diplomatic relations in the 1970s.

Tardigrades are tiny creatures that can survive in extreme conditions, even in space.

Tennessee and Missouri each share borders with eight states.

The 'Alphabet Song' and 'Twinkle Twinkle Little Star' have the same melody.

The 'sixth sick sheik's sixth sheep's sick' is believed to be the toughest tongue twister in the English language.

The 'G' on the Green Bay Packers helmet stands for 'greatness' not Green Bay!

The African continent has the most number of countries, totalling to 54 nations!

The age of most of the stars is between 1 and 10 billion years old.

The Amazon Rainforest produces 20% of the world's oxygen.

The American flag has 50 stars and 13 stripes, representing the states and original colonies.

The American lobster can live to be 20 years old.

The Atacama Desert, one of the driest places on Earth, blooms with flowers after rare rain.

The Atlantic Ocean is saltier than the Pacific Ocean.

The average brain weighs about three pounds. A newborn brain weighs about 3/4 of a pound.

The average cumulus cloud weighs about 1.1 million pounds.

The average person's left hand does 56% of the typing when using the proper position of the hands on the keyboard.

The average tongue is about three inches long.

The Aztecs built a great city called Tenochtitlan where Mexico City stands today.

The bald eagle has a wingspan of up to 8 feet.

The Berlin Wall, which separated East and West Berlin, fell in 1989.

The biggest and heaviest cheese ever created was 32 feet long and weighed 57,518 pounds! It required 540,000 pounds of milk!

The biggest fossil of a spider was found in China. It is one inch long and 165 million years old.

The biggest freshwater lake by surface area is Lake Superior. It is jointly shared by Canada and the USA and covers 82,100 square km.

The Brachiosaurus was so large it could eat leaves from treetops.

The Bristlecone pine trees in California can live for over 5,000 years.

The Brooklyn Bridge, completed in 1883, was the world's first steel-wire suspension bridge.

The capital of the United States is Washington, D.C.

The Catatumbo Lightning in Venezuela can create lightning storms that last for up to 10 hours.

The cheeseburger was reportedly invented in the U.S. in the 1920s.

The Coelacanth fish was thought to be extinct until found alive in 1938.

The colors of a rainbow always appear in the same order.

The Dinosaur Era: Dinosaurs lived during a period called the Mesozoic Era.

The dinosaur with the longest name is Micropachycephalosaurus.

The Diplodocus had a neck that was up to 20 feet long.

The double coconut palm produced the biggest seed in the world: 45 pounds.

The Earth acts like a giant magnet, which is why compasses point north.

The Earth's core is as hot as the surface of the sun.

The Elasmosaurus, a marine dinosaur, had a neck that was half the length of its body.

The Empire State Building in New York was once the tallest building in the world.

The English alphabet originally had only 24 letters; 'J' and 'U' were added later.

The Everglades in Florida is the largest tropical wilderness in the U.S.

The fastest recorded raindrop travelled at the speed of 18 mph!

The fastest tennis serve was recorded at 163.7 mph by Sam Groth in 2012.

The festive tradition of the Christmas tree dates back thousands of years to the Romans and Ancient Egyptians.

The Fibonacci sequence, a pattern found in nature, creates perfect spirals in sunflowers and pinecones.

The first crossword puzzle was created in 1913.

The first English dictionary was written in 1755.

The first Olympic Games were held in Greece in 776 BC.

The first Paralympic Games were held in Rome in 1960.

The first people to walk on the moon were American astronauts Neil Armstrong and Buzz Aldrin.

The first programmable computer, the Z3, was invented by Konrad Zuse in 1941.

The first recorded baseball game was in 1846 in Hoboken, New Jersey.

The first recorded use of a swear word in English was in 1475.
The first Super Bowl was held in 1967, and tickets cost only $6.

The first Winter Olympics were held in 1924 in Chamonix, France.

The first woman to go in space was Valentina Tereshkova in 1963! A Soviet cosmonaut, she spent more than 70 hours orbiting the Earth.

The footprints on the moon will be there for 100 million years.

The giant squid has the largest eyes in the world.

The Golden Gate Bridge in San Francisco was the longest suspension bridge span in the world when it was completed.

The Goliath frog from Western Africa can grow up to 16 inches long and weighs more than 7 pounds!

The Grand Canyon can fit the entire human population over 100 times.

The Grand Canyon of the USA is the largest canyon in the world.

The Great Lakes are the largest group of freshwater lakes on Earth by total area.

The Great Pyramid of Giza was the tallest man-made structure for over 3,800 years.

The Great Wall of China is so long that it would take about 18 months to walk its entire length.

The highest soccer score ever was 149-0 in a game in Madagascar in 2002.

The Hollywood Walk of Fame comprises over 2,600 five-pointed terrazzo and brass stars embedded in the sidewalks.

The human body has up to 206 bones.

The human brain uses the same amount of power as a 10-watt light bulb.

The largest living animal is the blue whale, which can measure as much as 100 feet.

The least sunny place is the South Pole, where the sun only shines on 182 days a year. (Which would you rather live in?)

The letter 'S' is used more often in plural forms than any other letter.

The letter 'Z' is the least used letter in the English language.

The Library of Alexandria in ancient Egypt was one of the largest and most significant libraries of the ancient world.

The Library of Congress is the largest library in the world.

The light we see from stars is actually many years old.

The longest cricket match ever lasted 14 days.

The longest golf hole is a par-7, 1,100-yard hole in South Korea.

The longest one-syllable words in the English language are 'scraunched' and 'strengthed.

The longest professional baseball game lasted 33 innings and over 8 hours.

The longest tennis match took 11 hours and 5 minutes over three days in 2010.

The longest word in English has 189,819 letters and describes a protein.

The loudest animal in the world is the Pistol Shrimp. It collapses its jaws so fast that it creates a sonic blast.

The Lyrebird can imitate almost any sound it hears, including chainsaws and camera shutters.

The marathon distance of 26.2 miles was set to match the distance from Marathon to Athens in Greece.

The Mississippi Delta region is known as the birthplace of the blues music genre.

The Mississippi River is the longest river in the U.S.

The moon can sometimes appear silver due to its reflective surface.

The moon is very hot (224 degrees Fahrenheit, average) during the day but very cold (-243 degrees average) at night.

The Moon's craters were created by asteroid impacts over billions of years.

The Morning Glory Pool in Yellowstone changes colors due to bacteria in the water.

The most common letter used in the English language is 'E.'

The most expensive book in the world was sold at a whopping price of $30.8 million to Bill Gates.

The most medals won for Olympic basketball (male or female) are by Teresa Edwards and Lisa Leslie with four gold medals each.

The most popular cheese recipe in America is Mac and Cheese.

The Naica Mine in Mexico has giant crystals, some as long as 36 feet.

The nation of Kiribati is the only country to cover all four hemispheres.

The National Aeronautics and Space Administration (NASA) is responsible for the nation's civilian space program.

The national bird of the United States is the bald eagle.

The national mammal of the United States is the American bison.

The Nile is the longest river in the world and is 6,600 km long.

The nose can detect a trillion smells!

The Olympics used to give medals for art, not just sports.

The opposite sides of the dice always add up to seven.

The original blue jeans were dyed with indigo, a natural blue dye.

The Pacific Ocean is the biggest and deepest ocean in the world. It can fit all the landmass into it! Crazy but true!

The Peacock Spider is known for its colorful patterns and unique mating dance.

The Pentagon in Virginia is one of the world's largest office buildings.

The place with the most rainfall on Earth is Mawsynram, India, receiving about 467 inches of rain per year.

The platypus is one of the few mammals that lays eggs.

The Pyramid of Khufu at Giza is the largest Egyptian pyramid and weighs as much as 16 Empire State buildings!

The Queen has two birthdays.

The QWERTY keyboard layout was designed to slow down typing to prevent typewriter jams.

The Rafflesia arnoldii is the largest flower in the world and smells like rotting flesh.

The record for the long jump is held by Mike Powell: 29 ft. + 4 inches. That's like jumping the length of two minivans!

The Red Sea is the saltiest sea in the world!

The rocks in the famous floating mountains in 'Avatar' were inspired by real mountains in China.

The Romans built roads so good that some are still used today.

The ruby is one of the few naturally red gemstones.

The Sahara desert in Africa is the largest hot desert in the world.

The shortest player in the National Hockey League (NHL) was goaltender Roy Waters who measured 5 ft. 3 in. tall.

The shortest war in history lasted just 38 minutes! It was between Britain and Zanzibar in 1896.

The shortest-serving president was William Henry Harrison, who was the ninth president of the United States for 31 days in 1841.

The smallest mammal on the Earth is Bumblebee Bat!

The so-called 'Walking Palm' in Central and South America can 'walk' by growing new roots.

The state of California has more people than the entire country of Canada.

The state which produces the most amount of cheese is Wisconsin. More than two and a half billion pounds are produced there every year.

The Statue of Liberty was a gift from France in 1886.

The Stegosaurus had spiked tail for defense which is called a thagomizer.

The strongest muscle in the body is the jaw.

The tallest monument in the United States is the Gateway Arch in St. Louis.

The tallest player in the NHL is Zdeno Chara, who is 6 ft. 9 in. tall.

The tallest tree in the world is a redwood named Hyperion, standing over 379 feet tall.

The term 'bookworm' comes from insects who live in and eat the binding of books.

The Titanic was the largest ship built at its time and sank on its maiden voyage in 1912.

The tomb of the young Egyptian pharaoh Tutankhamun was discovered almost entirely intact in 1922.

The Triceratops had three horns on its face for protection.

The Tyrannosaurus Rex had teeth as big as bananas!

The U.S. has 63 national parks.

The U.S. Independence Day is celebrated on July 4th.

The U.S. is the world's largest producer of corn.

The U.S. national anthem is "The Star-Spangled Banner."

The United States Capitol in Washington, D.C., is where the United States Congress meets.

The United States has the fourth-longest water system in the world.

The United States is made up of 50 states.

The United States was the birthplace of many inventions, including the light bulb and the internet.

The US gets over 1200 tornadoes a year.

The very first animals in space were fruit flies...they were sent up in 1947 and recovered alive.

The Vikings were excellent sailors and navigated their ships by the stars.

The Washington Monument is the tallest unreinforced stone masonry structure in the world.

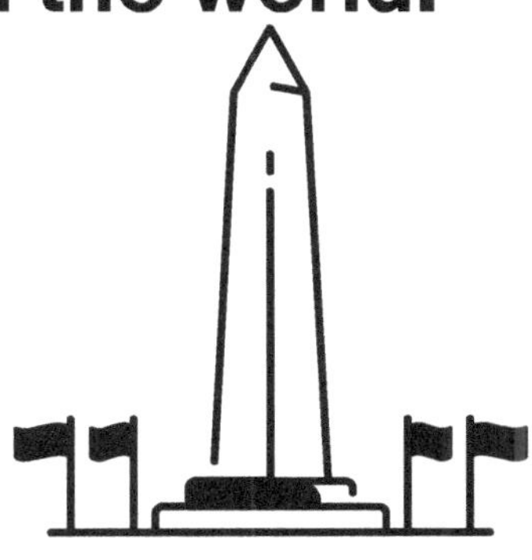

The wind is silent until it blows against something.

The word 'alphabet' comes from the first two letters of the Greek alphabet, alpha and beta.

The word 'Iouea' is a geological term and the shortest word in English that contains all five main vowels.

The word 'rhythms' is the longest English word without a vowel.

The world's largest brown bear, the Kodiak bear, lives in Alaska.

The world's largest chocolate bar weighed about 12,770 pounds, equivalent to the weight of a small elephant.

The world's highest waterfall is Angel Falls, Venezuela, South America. It is 979 m high!

The world's longest French fry is 34 inches long.

The Wright brothers made the first powered airplane flight in 1903.

The Wright Brothers only flew together once on May 25, 1910, in a six-minute flight piloted by Orville with Wilbur as his passenger.

The youngest Olympian ever was 10-year-old gymnast Dimitrios Loundras in 1896.

The youngest professional soccer player was 12 years old.

The Yucatan Peninsula in Mexico has a network of underground rivers.

There are 222 owl species in the world. Most are nocturnal, but a few are active during the daytime, such as the Barred Owl.

There are 293 ways to make change for a dollar.

There are 8 planets in our solar system.

There are a billion bacteria in your mouth at any time!

There are about 2,000 varieties of cheese.

There are about 60,000 miles of blood vessels in the human body.

There are ice caves in Iceland that have hot springs.

There are more stars in the universe than grains of sand on Earth.

There are more television sets in the United States of America than the number of people in the United Kingdom.

There are more than 1,000 kinds of bats in the world.

There are more than 8 million species of plants and animals on Earth, many of which haven't been discovered yet.

There are naturally purple vegetables like eggplants and purple carrots.

There are no male or female earthworms. All earthworms have both male and female parts.

There are only four words in the English language which end in 'dous': tremendous, horrendous, stupendous, and hazardous.

There are over 16,000 endangered species threatened with extinction.

There are places called 'magnetic hills' where cars seem to roll uphill due to an optical illusion.

There are starfish that have square bodies.

There are very few words in English that rhyme with 'orange.' There have been 46 presidents of the United States.

There is a sport called underwater hockey, which is played on the bottom of a swimming pool.

There is a type of apple called 'Ghost Apple' that is almost completely transparent.

There is enough gold in the Earth's oceans to turn every ocean blue-green.

There's a tree called the Rainbow Eucalyptus that has a multicolored trunk.

There's a type of algae that turns snow pink or watermelon-colored in certain parts of the world.

There's a type of ant in Malaysia that explodes to protect its colony.

There's a type of snow in Siberia that doesn't melt and is black instead of white.

There's an underwater waterfall illusion off the coast of Mauritius.

These animals have all been in outer space: chimpanzees, monkeys, dogs, mice, and a guinea pig.

Three of the nation's five founding fathers — John Adams, Thomas Jefferson and James Monroe — died on July 4th (Adams and Jefferson in 1826 and Monroe in 1831).

Thunder is the sound caused by lightning.

Tibetan Plateau, Asia is the world's highest and largest plateau. It is nearly four times the size of Texas!

Tigers are the largest wild cats in the world and can weigh up to 800 pounds.

Tigers have striped skin, not just striped fur.

Times Square in New York City is nicknamed 'The Crossroads of the World.'

Tiny but Terrifying: The smallest dinosaur was about the size of a chicken and called the Microraptor.

To get the orange color of cheddar cheese, flavorless Annatto seed is added.

Tomatoes and avocados are fruits, not vegetables.

Tomatoes are the most eaten fruit in the world.

Tornadoes can reach speeds of up to 300 miles per hour.

Trees can communicate and share nutrients through a network of fungi in their roots.

Tropical storms and hurricanes started getting 'named' in 1953.

Tug of war was an Olympic event between 1900 and 1920.

U.S. paper money is not made from paper; it's made from cotton and linen.

Usain Bolt holds the record for the fastest human, running at 27.8 mph.

Valles Marineris on Mars is the largest canyon in the solar system at nearly nine times longer and four times deeper than Grand Canyon.

Vatican City is the smallest country in the world.

Venus is the only planet that spins clockwise!

Volcanoes can shoot ash and lava miles into the air during an eruption.

Volleyball was invented in 1895, just four years after basketball.

Walruses can sleep while floating in water, thanks to air sacs in their throats that can function as inflatable pillows.

Walt Disney started sketching regularly when he was just four years old.

Water expands when it freezes, which is unusual for a liquid.

Water in space forms into floating balls due to zero gravity.

We don't know the exact colors of dinosaurs since their skin doesn't fossilize.

Wearing headphones for just an hour could increase the bacteria in your ear by 700 times.

Weird but true – At ancient Olympics, athletes performed naked!

Weird but true – Cockroaches have white blood!

Weird but true – Horses and cows can sleep lightly while standing up!

Weird but true – Nearly 75% of the human brain comprises of water!

Weird but true – Only male toads croak!

Weird but true – Russia spans 11 time zones!

Weird but true – The ancient Romans often used stale urine as mouthwash!! Yuck!!

Whales sleep vertically in the water.

While pandas sometimes eat fish or small animals, 99% of their diet is bamboo.

White As...: Polar bear fur is actually transparent, but it appears white.

White is the most popular car color.

Women first participated in the Olympics in the 1900 Paris games.

Women's hearts beat faster than men's.

Worms wiggle up from the ground when a flood is coming.

Wrestling and sprinting are considered the oldest sports.

Yellow Bananas? Not all bananas are yellow; some are red.

Yellowstone National Park was the world's first national park, established in 1872.

You can buy a piece of meteorite from eBay...Weird but true!

You can float in the Dead Sea because of its high salt content.

You can fry an egg on a hot sidewalk when it's reached 158 degrees Fahrenheit.

You can't breathe and swallow at the same time.

You can't smell anything while asleep!

You cannot walk on Jupiter, Neptune, Saturn or Uranus!! These planets are mostly made of gases and don't have a solid surface.

Your blood is as salty as the ocean.

Your heart beats about 115,000 times every day.

Your heart is about the same size as your fist.

Your left lung is about 10 percent smaller than your right lung.

Your mouth produces about 1 liter of saliva a day.

Your nose and ears never stop growing.

Your skin is the largest body organ!

Yuma, Arizona gets over 4000 hours of sunshine a year, making it the sunniest place on earth.

Zebras have unique stripes like human fingerprints, and their stripes may help repel insects.